Friends Help Me

Brenda Morris • Illustrated by **James Padgett**

Broadman Press
Nashville, Tennessee

ISBN: 0-8054-4179-4
Library of Congress Catalog Card Number: 86-18769
Dewey Decimal Classification: CE
Subject Heading: FRIENDSHIP

Printed in the United States of America

Library of Congress Cataloging-in-Publication Data

Morris, Brenda, 1943-
　Friends help me.

　(Bible-and-me)
　Summary: Emphasizes the value of having other people
who are kind and helpful and promotes discovery of ways
to be kind and loving to others.
　1. Friendship—Juvenile literature.　2. Love—
Juvenile literature.　3. Kindness—Juvenile literature.
[1. Kindness.　2. Conduct of life]　I. Padgett, Jim, ill.
II. Title.　III. Series.
BJ1533.F8M68　1987　158'.25　86-18769
ISBN 0-8054-4179-4

Who helps Jessica? Daddy helps Jessica. He helps Jessica put on her shoes.

Mother helps Jessica. Mother makes pancakes for breakfast. Jessica likes pancakes.

Jessica is a helper too. Jessica helps set the table. "You are a good helper, Jessica," Mother says.

Randy is Jessica's brother. Randy and
Jessica play with the ball. Jessica rolls the
ball to Randy.

Who helps Jessica? Grandma and Grandpa
help Jessica. "We are glad to see you,
Jessica," Grandma and Grandpa say.

Grandpa and Jessica are helpers. Grandpa carries groceries. Jessica carries groceries too.

Grandma makes cookies. Jessica helps
Grandma. She puts raisins in the dough.

Grandpa, Grandma, and Jessica eat the
cookies. Jessica is glad for Grandma and
Grandpa and the cookies.

Who is Jessica's friend? Jessica sees the mail carrier. He brings the mail.

Who helps Jessica? Grandpa helps Jessica
reach the mailbox. Jessica can carry the
mail into the house.

Grandma helps Jessica put cookies in a
sack. "You may take these home,"
Grandma tells Jessica.

Who is Jessica's friend? Mr. Smith is
Jessica's friend. He lives next door. He helps
Jessica find her puppy.

Jessica is a helper too. She gives her puppy
a drink. Jessica likes to be a helper.

Who is Jessica's friend. Mrs. Jones is
Jessica's friend. She helps Jessica read a
book.

Jessica gives a flower to Mrs. Jones. "Thank you, Jessica," says Mrs. Jones. "I like flowers."

Who are Jessica's friends at church. Mrs.
Watts is a friend at church. She helps
Jessica work a puzzle.

Mr. Vincent is a friend at church. He helps Jessica and other boys and girls. He helps them sing.

Mr. Vincent plays the autoharp. He helps
Jessica. She can play the autoharp too.

Pastor Franks is Jessica's friend. Jessica
shows Pastor Franks her painting.

"I am glad you came to church, Jessica,"
Pastor Franks says.

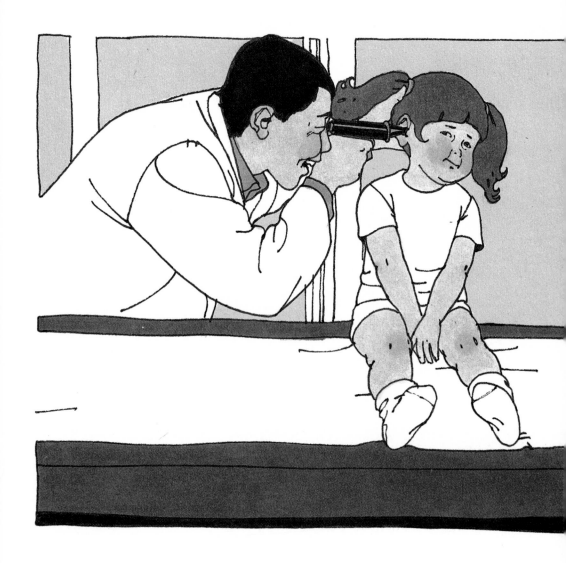

Who is Jessica's friend? Doctor Yim is
Jessica's friend. He helps Jessica when she is
sick.

Doctor Yim sees Jessica for a check-up when she is well. Nurse Kelly is Jessica's friend too.

Nurse Kelly helps Jessica. She helps Jessica weigh. She helps Jessica know how much she grows.

Who is Jessica's friend? Jane is Jessica's babysitter. She stays with Jessica while Mother goes shopping.

Jessica has fun with Jane.

Jane helps Jessica go down the slide. Jessica likes to slide.

Sometimes Jessica falls and skins her knee.
Jane helps Jessica then.

Jessica is glad Jane is her friend.

"My friends help me," Jessica says. "You have many friends," say Mother and Daddy. "Many people help you."